Famous
Illustrated Tales of
INDIAN MYTHOLOGY

MAPLE KIDS

Famous Illustrated Tales of
INDIAN MYTHOLOGY

Published by

MAPLE PRESS PRIVATE LIMITED

Corporate & Editorial Office
A 63, Sector 58, Noida 201 301, U.P., India

phone: +91 120 455 3581, 455 3583
email: info@maplepress.co.in
website: www.maplepress.co.in

Reprint 2020

ISBN: 978-93-50339-15-2

Printed at HT Media Ltd, Gr. Noida, India

10 9 8 7 6 5 4

Contents

King Manu and the Fish

Many years ago, King Manu, a noble man ruled the earth. It is said that he was the first ruler of the earth. He was a man of great wisdom and was devoted to virtue. King Manu had been engaged in severe penance for thousands of years. On one fine day he went to a river near his palace to offer his prayers when he collected a tiny fish in his cupped hands, along with water by mistake. The king was

about to let the fish escape into the river again when the fish spoke, "Great king, do not throw me away. Keep me with you. I shall be of help to you some day."

The king was highly pleased by the fish's request. So he brought the fish home. The king put the tiny fish in a jar. For a few days the fish remained happily in the jar. But then one day the king noticed that the fish was unable to move in the jar. It had grown so much that there was hardly any space in the jar. It made the fish very unhappy. So the king took pity on the fish and shifted it to a tank. For some days the fish remained happy in the tank but again it had grown so much that now it hardly had any room to move within the tank.

So the king threw the fish in a lake. Its joy knew no bounds. It jumped and played in the lake. But in a few days the fish had grown again and now the lake was too small for it. When the king came to visit it he was shocked to see the fish so unhappy again. So he arranged some men to transfer the fish from the lake to a river. But in few days even the river proved to be too small for the fish.

The king realized that it was no ordinary fish. He bowed to the fish and said, "I now understand that you are no ordinary fish but a lord. Bless me that I may run my kingdom with more justice and wisdom. Bless us that peace may always prevail in our land."

The fish said, "Great king, I am satisfied with your service towards me. I have come to warn you that in a few days it will start raining heavily. The rain will continue for the next seven days and there would be a huge flood that will drown the whole earth. You must build a big ship and fill it with good people, animals and plants of all kind and set sail."

Though this prediction surprised King Manu, he did not say anything and decided to obey the fish's order. He immediately set off to build a huge ship and filled it with all kinds of animals, plants and the good people. When it began to rain and the land was drowned by the ocean, he set sail in his ship.

For seven days it rained heavily and they sailed through the storms. But the ship did not sink. Do you know why? It was because the giant fish was carrying the ship on its back. This giant fish was Matsya, an *avatar* of Lord Vishnu.

When the raining stopped and the flood was over, King Manu's ship came ashore and all the animals, plants and good men who were on it, were saved. Together with them, King Manu then created a new kingdom and a new era started.

Nectar of Immortality

While the Asuras, the Daityas and the Gods were fighting over who should get the largest share of the nectar of immortality called *amrita*, Lord Vishnu thought, "If the Asuras and the Daityas become immortal by drinking the *amrita*, then they would continue to create troubles for all those who live on the earth and in the heavens. There would be no way left to stop them. I must do something so that they do not get to drink the *amrita*."

Lord Vishnu quietly turned himself into a lovely

maiden and stepped out of the ocean. No sooner had she appeared, all the Asuras, the Daityas and the Gods stopped fighting and they gazed at her in surprise. A bright light had lit up the sky and from within it stepped out the divine beauty.

The maiden said, "My name is Mohini." Her voice was so sweet that it sounded like a song. Now the Gods and the Daityas had understood that Mohini had appeared from the churning of the ocean. The fight resumed, and this time it was for who should keep Mohini for themselves.

Then Mohini said, "I would like to offer a solution if you agree. That way both the parties can enjoy me and the *amrita* equally." Mohini was so charming that the Gods and the Daityas could hardly refuse her offer. She continued, "Give me the pot containing the *amrita* and I will divide it amongst you equally." Since Mohini was neither a God nor a Daitya or Asura, everyone trusted that she would be fair and so they agreed.

Mohini began to dance with the pot of *amrita* in her hand. What a charming performer she was! All the Gods and the Asuras and the Daityas were stunned to see her graceful moves. They sat awestruck and looked at her while Mohini distributed the *amrita*.

The clever maiden magically exchanged the pot of *amrita* with a pot of water while she danced so that the Gods drank from the real pot while the Asuras and the Daityas got to drink from the fake one. So, all the Gods became immortal as they drank the *amrita*. Meanwhile the Asuras and Daityas were tricked as they drank water instead of the nectar of immortality.

One of the Asuras named Rahu realized what was happening. So to check whether Mohini

was cheating on the Asuras and the Daityas, he
disguised himself as a God and went and sat
between the Sun and the Moon Gods. Mohini did
not realize this. As she danced she reached Rahu
and offered him the nectar.

Rahu took a sip of the nectar and his doubts
were confirmed that Mohini had been cheating
the Asuras and the Daityas by offering them water
instead of *amrita*. On the other hand, the Sun and
the Moon realized that Rahu was not a God but an
Asura in disguise they shouted, "He is not a God but
an Asura, he is cheating!"

This enraged Rahu. He began to grow in size.
He opened his mouth and swallowed the Sun and

the Moon because they had revealed out his secret.
Mohini turned back into her original *avatar* and
there, to everyone's astonishment, Lord Vishnu
stood in place of the beautiful Mohini. With his
sudarshan chakra—the divine discus, Lord Vishnu
then cut Rahu's head from his body and the Sun and
the Moon, whom the Asura had swallowed escaped
from his throat.

Because Rahu had already taken a sip of the
nectar of immortality, he did not die. But his head
was separated from his body for ever. Thus, his
head is known as Rahu while his body began to be
called as Ketu. To this day Rahu continues to take
his revenge by swallowing the Sun and the Moon
causing what we call as the eclipse. But because
he is just a severed head, the Sun and the Moon
continue to escape from his throat, causing the
eclipse to end within minutes.

Varaha Avatar

Long long ago, Lord Brahma created four boys and blessed them to live as eternal boysaints. These four saints were named Sanaka, Sanandana, Sanatana and Sanathkumara. The four boys had miraculous powers. Once, they decided to visit Lord Vishnu. After getting the permission and blessings from their father Lord Brahma, the four saints set out for the abode of Lord Vishnu at Vaikuntha.

Vaikuntha has seven gates. The four saints crossed six gates but were stopped at the seventh gate by Jay and Vijay. The two of them did not let them enter this last gate. Being saints they wore only their loincloth. Jay and Vijay insulted them saying that they were not even properly dressed. The four of them reminded Jay and Vijay that they were sons of Brahma. But Jay and Vijay did not listen. They accused the four boys of creating a scene and threatened that they will be thrown out of Vaikuntha. This insult was too much. The four boys got so angry that they cursed Jay and Vijay to be born as demons on the earth as they were too arrogant to be in such a sacred place. The whole Vaikuntha trembled due to their rage.

Jay and Vijay realized their mistake, but it was too late. At this moment Lord Vishnu appeared along

with Goddess Lakshmi. Lord Vishnu said, "Your behaviour was unpardonable. Never before had the four saints cursed anybody. Hence, their curse must take effect."

Jay and Vijay then fell at the feet of the four saints. They begged for mercy. Feeling pity for the gatekeepers, they said, "Your curse cannot be removed but be assured that there will be happiness before it ends. You shall be born on the earth only three times and will be killed by Lord Vishnu every time. Thereby, you shall attain salvation and return to this abode."

Thus, Jay and Vijay were born on the earth for the first time as the demon brothers, Hiranyakashyap and Hiranyaksh. It is said that when they were born, both the earth and the heavens shook. All the Gods were afraid that if while being born they were so ferocious, what would happen when they grow up.

Years went by and Hiranyaksh grew to be a devotee of Lord Brahma. After devoting himself for thousands of years in hard penance, Lord Brahma appeared to him and promised to bless him with a wish. Hiranyaksh said, "Lord, bless me that I may never be killed by any human, God or demon." Brahma granted his wish and disappeared.

After this Hiranyaksh, the demon king ruled like a tyrant the world had never seen. He was so confident of his immortality that he started to disturb the peace upon the earth. First he stood in the middle of the ocean and moved his waist from side to side. This churned the waters much to the sorrow of the Water God Varun. When he appeared, Hiranyaksh challenged Varun to a duel. Varun had no choice but to agree. But since Hiranyaksh was blessed by Brahma, Varun could not defeat him. He went to Lord Vishnu to ask for his help.

Meanwhile, having defeated Varun, Hiranyaksh's confidence grew to manifolds. He took the earth and began sinking into the ocean to reach the *patallok*. This worried all the other Gods and they joined Varun and prayed to Lord Vishnu for help.

Lord Vishnu then took the *avatar* of a wild boar and went to *patallok* in search of Hiranyaksh. He found the demon king sitting there with the earth on his knee. The boar challenged Hiranyaksh for a fight. Proud Hiranyaksh agreed. But he had forgotten that he had asked Brahma to bless him with the ability to only win over a human, God or demon. Brahma's blessing did not work because Hiranyaksh was fighting with an animal now. So the boar easily defeated Hiranyaksh and after it had killed him it brought the earth back from the *patallok* and restored peace.

This *avatar* which the Lord Vishnu had taken to kill Hiranyaksh is known as Varaha Avatar. Thus, as Hiranyaksh was killed by Lord Vishnu's Varaha Avatar, the gatekeeper was set free from the curse as the four saints had predicted.

Narasimha Avatar

When Hiranyaksh's brother Hiranyakashyap heard of his brother's death he was filled with anger. He swore revenge against Lord Vishnu. He went to the Mandrachal mountain, stood on one toe and did penance for hundred years until Brahma appeared before him. Brahma said, "I am really pleased by your penance. You may now ask for a boon."

Hiranyakashyap said, "Lord, bless me that I am not killed by any weapons. Nor will I be killed by any human or animal, Daitya, Asura or God. Bless me lord that I will neither die in the day or at night, neither outside nor inside, neither in the sky nor on the earth."

Brahma granted Hiranyakashyap his wish and from that day, he rose to be as tyrant as his brother for he knew he was immortal. He waged a war and won all the kingdoms on the earth. He declared that everyone on earth must worship him as he was the most powerful amongst all Gods and Asuras. Everyone under his rule feared him, so no one dared to disobey his orders.

But Hiranyakashyap had a son called Prahlad. Young Prahlad remained the only one who devoted himself to Lord Vishnu instead of worshipping his father like everybody. He sang praises of Lord Vishnu which annoyed his father very much. So,

Hiranyakashyap sent Prahlad to the best master in the city. But in a few days the master came back complaining that instead of mending his ways Prahlad had convinced all his friends to worship Lord Vishnu.

Hiranyakashyap was so angry that he ordered the guards to throw Prahlad from a cliff. The guards captured Prahlad. They felt sorry for the poor boy but they could not disobey their king. So they threw Prahlad from a high cliff. Then a miracle happened. The fall did not even give Prahlad a scratch. He stood at the bottom of the cliff and said, "Lord Vishnu is the most powerful. Lord Vishnu is the most kind."

Hiranyakashyap's anger grew when his guards told him about what had happened. He had a sister

who was called Holika. Holika said, "Brother, I have a boon that I will not be burnt by fire. If you permit, I would sit in a pyre with Prahlad on my lap. The boy would be burnt to ashes within minutes." The king agreed and a pyre was arranged. Holika sat with Prahlad on it and it was lit. But then another miracle happened. Holika began to scream as her boon failed. She got burnt to ashes as nothing happened to Prahlad. He safely sat in the fire and chanted Lord Vishnu's name. Hiranyakashyap bellowed, "If you think your God is so powerful let him fight me. I challenge him to defeat me. Where is your lord? Is he hiding somewhere, afraid of me?" Prahlad said, "Father, Lord Vishnu is never afraid. He is all powerful. He is everywhere." Hiranyakashyap said, "Everywhere? Is he in this pillar too?" Prahlad said, "Yes father. He is in that pillar."

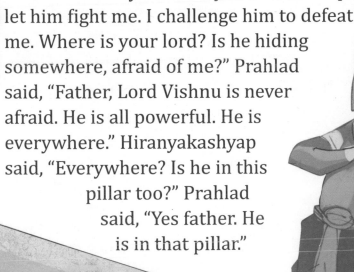

Hiranyakashyap punched the pillar and it crumbled on the ground. From within it stepped out a large man with a lion's face. It roared loudly and lifted Hiranyakashyap over his head with both his hands. He was so powerful that Hiranyakashyap at once knew, he was no match for this man-lion. The half man, half lion then took the evil king to the door and sat down at the threshold. He placed the king on his knees and tore his chest apart with his claws as the sun was about to set. Hiranyakashyap died because he was placed neither inside nor outside but at the door. It was neither a man nor an animal which killed him and no weapon was used, for the man-lion used his claws. It was neither day nor night, for it was evening, and he died on the knees on the man-lion which was neither the earth nor the sky.

Prahlad bowed to the man-lion for he was Lord Vishnu. We know this half-man half-lion form of Lord Vishnu as the Narasimha Avatar. Hiranyakashyap after being killed by Lord Vishnu returned to Lord Vishnu's abode and as the curse laid upon him by the four saints broke, he came back to his original form as the gatekeeper.

Savitri and Satyavan

Long ago in India, there was a king who had no children. He would often worry about what will happen to his kingdom after he died. He needed an heir. He worshipped many Gods and performed many sacrificial rites for a child. But it was all in vain. But one day, Goddess Savitri came to him in his dreams and said that she was happy with his devotion. She said she would present him with a daughter.

Soon the king and his queen were blessed with a daughter. The king's happiness knew no bounds. He named her Savitri, after the Goddess. The king and the queen loved their daughter very much. So Savitri grew up to be a very beautiful and intelligent young woman.

When she was of age, her parents decided to get her married to a suitable young prince. But it was difficult to find a man worthy of their daughter. So Savitri said, "Father, let me travel across the kingdom and find a husband for myself." So she left the palace, dressed as a commoner and began to travel all around the city.

She travelled for many months and finally

reached a hermitage. The hermitage was within a forest and so it was a peaceful place. Savitri decided to spend some days here. As she went about her daily chores, Savitri noticed a very handsome young man taking care of a blind old man. She asked the eldest sage in the hermitage about them. The wise old sage said, "The young man you see is a prince. His name is Satyavan. The blind old man is his father. They have lost their kingdom to another king and are now forced to live in this hermitage. The king lost his eyesight with age but to see the prince still caring for his father warms our hearts."

Savitri decided that she would marry Satyavan. She came back to her palace and told her parents about it. Both the king and the queen were very happy. They rode to the hermitage with the marriage proposal.

The blind king was very happy to receive Savitri's father. Satyavan too accepted the proposal gladly. But when their horoscopes were matched, the sages warned that Satyavan was supposed to die within a year. Nevertheless, Savitri married Satyavan for she had already chosen him as her husband. She said that she would rather spend one year with Satyavan than spend the rest of her life with another man.

In the months that followed, Satyavan and Savitri were married. Savitri left behind the luxurious life she had as a princess and came to live in the hermitage with Satyavan. Though she was very happy, she feared for her husband's life as the year came to an end.

On his last day, Satyavan went to chop some wood from the forest when he felt dizzy and fell down on the ground. When Savitri found him she ran to him and sat with his head on her lap. There was nothing she could do as Satyavan lay with his eyes closed. She began to grieve for her husband.

Suddenly Lord Yama, the God of death came to them. With his noose he captured Satyavan's soul and began to leave. Savitri begged, "I pray to you lord, please let my husband go." Lord Yama tried to console

Savitri. He said, "Child, Satyavan was a man of great virtue and happiness awaits him in my kingdom."

Savitri did not say anything but rose and started following Yama. Yama said, "You cannot follow me to the land of the dead!" Savitri replied, "Lord, I know you are doing your duty of taking away the soul of my husband when it is time. But my duty as his wife is to stay beside him."

Yama said, "Your duty is over as your husband is dead. But I admire your loyalty. I will grant a wish of yours. Tell me what do you desire? But do not ask for your husband's life." Savitri said, "Please return the kingdom my husband and his father had lost along with my father-in-law's eyesight."

Lord Yama granted Savitri's wish and moved on. He began to walk through thorny bushes. Savitri continued to follow him. Her clothes tore and her feet began to bleed. Yama said, "Go back child, you mustn't follow me." Savitri said, "Lord Yama, my husband will find happiness in your kingdom but you are carrying away the happiness that is mine."

Yama said, "I admire your devotion. I will grant you another wish." Savitri said, "I am my father's only child. He has been unhappy since I got married and left him. I pray you give him many more children." Yama granted her wish. He then began to climb a steep slope. Savitri followed. It made her tired but she did not stop.

Yama said, "I forbid you to come farther. I am telling
for the last time that you have come far enough. I
admire your courage and your firmness. I grant you
one last favour, anything, but the life of your husband."

Savitri said, "Please grant me that I have many
children with Satyavan." Yama was surprised at
this wish. Savitri had not asked for her husband's
life but he was forced to release Satyavan's soul.
Savitri found that she was sitting in the forest with
her husband's head on her lap. Satyavan opened
his eyes. Seeing that Savitri had tears in her eyes he
asked, "What happened?" Savitri shook her head
and smiled. They lived happily for a very long time.

Brave Dhruva's Devotion

Once upon a time there was a king named Uttanapada. He had two queens, Suniti and Suruchi. Each of the queens had a son. Suniti's son was named Dhruva and Suruchi's son was named Uttama. The king loved his second queen Suruchi more. So Uttama was his favourite son.

One day Dhruva saw that Uttama was sitting on their father's lap and playing. He too wished to sit on his father's lap. He went to his father and said, "Father, take me onto your lap too. I also want to play with you." But his stepmother Suruchi said, "You are not so lucky because you were not born as my son. Only my son is allowed to sit on the king's lap. Go and pray to Lord Vishnu that you be born as my son in your next life."

These harsh words of his stepmother hurt Dhruva a lot. He went weeping to Suniti. He told her everything that had happened. Suniti was also very hurt to hear it. But she consoled her son saying, "Do not worry child. Lord Vishnu is great. He loves all of us. He will take care of you." Dhruva asked if Lord Vishnu was greater than his father. His mother said that indeed he was. Dhruva decided that he would go to find Lord Vishnu. No matter how much his mother tried to stop him, Dhruva was determined.

So, ten-year-old Dhruva left his palace and went into the forest in search of Lord Vishnu. He began to spend his days eating wild berries and sleeping on the trees. He walked in the forest for many days when he met Narada Muni. Narada asked, "What is a

little boy like you doing in a dangerous forest as this?" Dhruva told him that he was looking for Lord Vishnu. Narada said, "I am afraid, you won't be able to find the lord by just wandering in the forest. You will have to do penance for it. It is only those who please the lord with their devotion, are able to see him." Dhruva said, "I am ready to do penance. Tell me what I have to do to please the lord?"

Narada said, "Penance is not for innocent children like you. Even men have failed to do it. You must sit by a certain tree beside river Yamuna and chant the lord's name for years, without food or water, without sleep or exercise." Dhruva thanked Narada for his advice and went to the tree beside river Yamuna.

There he sat chanting "Om Namah Narayana". Years passed but Dhruva did not move.

Finally, one day Lord Vishnu appeared before him. Dhruva opened his eyes and bowed to the lord. He had wanted to ask many question to the lord when he had begun his penance. But now when the lord was before him he realized how unimportant those questions were. Lord Vishnu said, "Child, I am very pleased by your devotion. Tell me what do you wish for?"

Dhruva said, "Lord I had only wished to see you. Now that you are here, I have no more desires." Lord Vishnu was impressed. He said, "Your devotion and wisdom is great. I hereby grant you that till the time stars shine in the sky, your fame will shine over the world. All the stars will move around you. You will guide travellers from the sky when they have lost their paths."

Dhruva returned home to his parents. He was welcomed by the people of his city. After his father's death, Dhruva ruled his kingdom with justice and proved to be a great king. When he died, he became the brightest star in the sky. Even today we can see the *dhruvatara* fixed at the North Pole, guiding travellers with its light.

Bhasmasur

Once, a mighty Asura did penance for hundreds of years in order to satisfy Lord Shiva. He went deep into the forest and sat under a tree and chanted Lord Shiva's name. Lord Shiva was finally satisfied and he appeared before Bhasmasur. He said, "I am very pleased with your devotion. Tell me, what is it that you want?"

Bhasmasur replied, "Lord, bless me that I may become immortal." Lord Shiva said, "I cannot make you immortal. Ask me for something else." So Bhasmasur said, "Then bless me lord, that no sooner I have placed my hand on someone's head then he may be turned into ashes."

Lord Shiva had no choice but to grant the evil Bhasmasur his wish. Bhasmasur was glad. He knew no one would be able to defeat him. He began to create havoc on earth. The evil demon killed many people. When he was tired of killing people he began to chase Gods.

Unable to defeat Bhasmasur the Gods went to Lord Vishnu for his help. They said, "Lord, it is impossible to stop Bhasmasur. He has been killing men and threatening Gods with his boon. This way he will soon win over all of heaven and earth." Lord Vishnu asked them not to worry. He transformed into Mohini and went to Bhasmasur.

Mohini was so beautiful that Bhasmasur could not take his eyes off her. He said to Mohini, "I pray to you, marry me. I have fallen in love with your beauty." Mohini blushed and said, "I cannot marry you. You are an ugly demon. You are no match for me." Bhasmasur was so blinded by love that he was ready to do anything for it. He said, "Marry me sweet woman, I shall do anything for you." Mohini said, "All right, on one condition. If you are a good dancer, I will marry you." He said he would prove it to Mohini that he was a great dancer. Mohini said, "I will dance. If you can match every step of yours to mine I will marry you." Bhasmasur agreed.

The dancing began. Mohini danced and so danced Bhasmasur. While dancing, Mohini placed her hand on her waist. Bhasmasur also placed his hand on his waist. Then Mohini placed her hand on her shoulder. Bhasmasur followed her. Then Mohini placed her hand on her nose. Bhasmasur also placed his hand on his nose. She touched her cheek, so did Bhasmasur.

They danced tirelessly for a very long time. Whatever Mohini did Bhasmasur did his best to match his steps to hers and so he copied her. He was so madly in love with her that he forgot all about his boon. Mohini took the opportunity and she placed her hand on her head. But no sooner

Bhasmasur had copied her and placed his hand on his head, he was turned into ashes.

Bhasmasur died and all the Gods heaved a sigh of relief. Thus, Mohini who had previously tricked the Daityas and the Asuras while she distributed the nectar of immortality, tricked Bhasmasur this time who turned himself into ashes when he placed his hand on his own head. Mohini changed in her original form. There over Bhasmasur's ashes stood Lord Vishnu. Flowers began pouring from the heavens, over him.

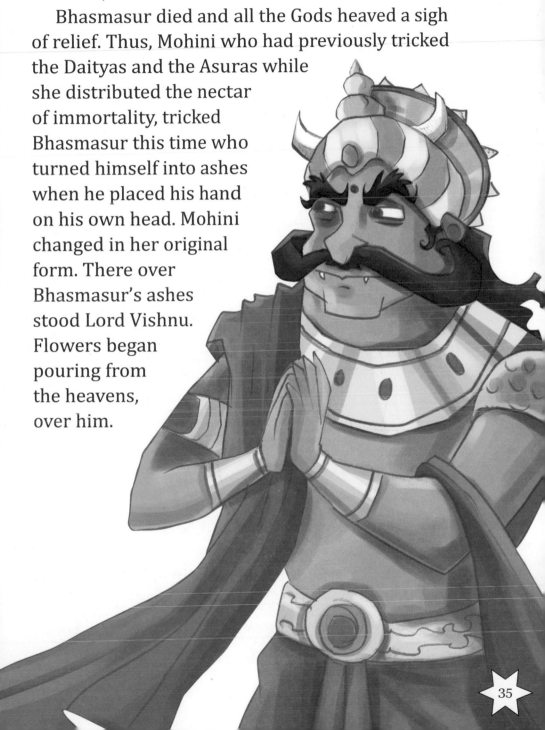

The Govardhan Hill

Lord Krishna had saved the people of Braj from the severe rains that lasted for seven days by sheltering them under the Govardhan hill.

Once upon a time in Braj, people were desperately praying to Lord Indra, the God of Rains. It had not rained for many years. They made all necessary offerings to Lord Indra but it had no effect. So Lord Krishna persuaded the people to stop worshipping Lord Indra. He said, "Hills, trees and rivers should be worshipped for rains. Pray to Mount Govardhan. He would surely bring in the rains."

The people of Braj started to worship Mount Govardhan and Lord Krishna joined them. This made Lord Indra very angry. He felt that he was insulted and the fact that he had lost his gifts made him decide to take revenge. He thought, "How dare these milkmen and shepherds insult me? I will teach them such a lesson that they will remember all their lives."

Lord Indra summoned the Samvartaka. They were the dark clouds and he showered torrents of rain on the earth. Braj began to drown as Samvartaka fell on it as large heavy drops and flooded the rivers and lakes. The thunderstorms and lightening awoke fear in the hearts of the poor people. The strong winds uprooted the trees and destroyed the houses.

The people ran to Lord Krishna. They said, "O Krishna, only you can save us. If the rain continues, we will all die along with our cattle and herd." Lord Krishna knew that this untimely storm was a wrong doing of Lord Indra. He had to do something to save his people and destroy Indra's pride.

He concentrated all his strength into his little finger. Then going to the Govardhan hill, he lifted the hill up and placed it on his little finger. Everyone was surprised.

"Get your families, cattle and herd. We shall stay under this hill until the storms pass. Do not worry, you shall all be safe as Govardhan will not fall on you." Everyone rushed to take shelter under the mighty Govardhan. It rained for almost seven days but not a single drop fell on Govardhan hill as it sheltered every single man and animal of Braj under it.

Lord Krishna held the hill on his little finger for the time it rained, without wavering even for once. Lord Indra was amazed at the young Lord Krishna's determination. He was

forced to give up in the end and the raining stopped after seven days.

The next day, when Lord Krishna with his brother Balarama went to graze the cows in the field, Lord Indra came down on the celestial elephant Eravat and begged for an apology from Lord Krishna. He had realized his mistake. Everyone in Braj rejoiced after the rains were over. From that day on, people of Braj worshipped Govardhan hill as their protector. Govardhan is loved and respected so much that people call it Giriraj or King of hills. Today, Shri Krishna as Shri Giridhari or the holder of hills graces the devotees at Nathdwara in Rajasthan.

Sudama

Sudama was a poor *brahmin* boy who became a close friend of Krishna in Sage Sandipani's hermitage. It is said that little Lord Krishna learnt to chant from Sudama.

Once, Sage Sandipani asked them to get some wood from the forest to light the stove. So Krishna and Sudama went to the forest together. But a terrible storm arose as they were collecting the wood. Sudama began to worry, but Krishna held his hands and assured him that nothing bad will happen to them. When the storm was past, they carried their bundle of wood back home. Krishna never left Sudama's side in the forest and Sudama thanked God secretly for such a kind friend.

After completing their studies, Sudama and Krishna went their own ways. Sandipani blessed them with a long life and happiness. Krishna became the king of Dwarka and married princess Rukmini, the Goddess of prosperity. Sudama married a simple *brahmin* girl and began to lead the life of a devotee. He read the scriptures and prayed. He had forsaken all worldly pleasures. Everyone loved Sudama for he was kind and gentle. For some time he lived happily with his wife.

Then Sudama's wife gave birth to two children. As Sudama lived a very simple life it was now difficult for him to provide enough food or clothes for everyone in his family. Sudama's wife was very devoted to her husband but when she saw that her children were suffering because of their poverty she begged her husband to visit his friend Krishna and ask for help. Sudama replied, "How can I possibly go to Krishna asking for help. He is the king of the great city of Dwarka. I am a humble *brahmin* and hardly a match for him. I am not eligible to call myself his friend."

But Sudama's wife continued to pester him. Finally, Sudama gave in and said, "All right, I will go and pay Krishna a visit. But what do we have that I can offer him as a present? We do not have even a grain of food or a thread of cloth for ourselves."

His wife said, "I remember you had once said that Krishna loved flattened rice. I will go and ask our neighbour to lend me some." So she went to their neighbour and got a handful of flattened rice from her. Tying it in a piece of cloth she gave it to Sudama and got him to set off for Dwarka.

Sudama walked through the forest for many days. Then he came upon the heavy gates of the great city. They were made of gold and gleamed in the sunshine. Sudama was about to enter the gate when the gatekeeper stopped him. He asked, "What is the purpose of your visit?" Sudama said, "I have come to see king Krishna." The gatekeeper laughed. He said, "And why do you think our king would want to see a poor *brahmin* like you?" Sudama said, "Because I am his friend." The gatekeeper laughed and laughed.

But nevertheless, the gatekeeper went to Krishna and informed him about Sudama. He said, "Your majesty, there is a poor *brahmin* standing at the doors of this city. He must be mad for he says he is your friend. He calls himself Sudama."

But when Krishna heard this he leaped from his throne, ran barefooted through the streets and reached the gate. He welcomed Sudama with tears of happiness. He said, "Where had you been dear friend. I have missed you so much." Sudama too was happy to meet Krishna. He was surprised that Krishna had come to receive him.

When Sudama reached Krishna's palace he was amazed at the prosperity. The palace walls gleamed with precious stones and gold. Krishna took Sudama inside and washed his feet with rose water. They talked about many things.

When it was time for Sudama to go, Krishna noticed that his friend was carrying some flattened rice in a piece of cloth. Krishna said,

"Is that little bundle for me?" Sudama seemed very embarrassed. He did not say anything. Krishna snatched the bundle and opened it. He then tossed some flatten rice into his mouth and chewed with satisfaction.

Sudama bid Krishna farewell and set off for home. He couldn't bring himself to tell Krishna about his wretched condition and ask for help. All through the way he kept thinking about the kindness Krishna had shown him. He felt very proud to have such a friend.

When Sudama reached home, he witnessed a miracle. His little hut had converted into a mansion and his children now played in the large courtyard. They were wearing new clothes and were very happy. His wife ran to him when she noticed him at the gate. She said, "Isn't this marvellous?"

Sudama silently nodded. He had understood that only Krishna could have been so powerful and generous to do this for him. Tears rolled down from his eyes as he thanked Lord Krishna in his heart.

Arjuna and the Bird's Eye

Once, on a bright sunny morning, a large group of young boys had gathered in a field by a small stream. They all carried their bows and arrows. These young boys were none other than the Pandavas and the Kauravas.

The five Pandava brothers and hundred Kaurava brothers were cousins, and a fierce rivalry between them began when they were only children. The military expert of their court Dronacharya was their teacher who had decided to organize a competition between the princes.

As the young princes gathered in the field, Dronacharya set up a small wooden bird in a tree across the stream. He said, "I want to see who among you can strike the eye of that wooden bird across the river." Everyone was surprised as the bird appeared tiny from where they were standing. But the boys were confident that they could pass their teacher's test. Anxiously

the young princes stood waiting for Dronacharya
to call their names. Yudhisthira, the eldest among
the Pandavas was called first. Taking his position
he placed his arrow on the bow and drew it taut.
Dronacharya asked, "Tell me Yudhisthira, what do
you see?"

Wanting to impress his teacher, Yudhisthira
began to list everything he could see. He said,
"Master, I can see the bird, the branch, other birds
on that branch, the tree, the bank, the stream, the
clouds, the sky, the sun..."

Dronacharya raised his hand to make

Yudhisthira stop. Then he said, "Lower your bow. You will not be able to hit the bird's eye." Surprised, Yudhisthira lowered his bow. Dronacharya called the other princes. One by one everyone tried their hand at shooting the bird's eye. Dronacharya asked each of them the same question and just like Yudhisthira, they all began to list everything that they saw around them.

Just as he had asked Yudhisthira to lower his bow, Dronacharya asked all of them to lower theirs as he said that their arrows would fail to hit the bird's eye.

At last it was Arjuna's turn. Dronacharya asked him the question that he had been asking all his students. He said, "Tell me son, what do you see?" Arjuna pulled his bowstring taut and placed his arrow over it, ready for release. He said, "I can see only the eye."

Dronacharya said, "Do you not see the bird, or the tree or the grass or the clouds?" Arjuna said, "No master, I can see only the eye." Dronacharya smiled. He commanded, "Shoot."

Arjuna who was holding his bow steady till now let go of the arrow. It was a perfect shot. The bird fell with a small thud as all the boys looked on in amazement at Arjuna. The arrow had hit its eye.

Dronacharya was pleased. He cast a glance at his students. They slowly began nodding as the lesson became clear to them. Dronacharya was happy that one of his favourite students was able to pass his test. He patted Arjuna on the back and said, "Now you see, young princes, success lies only in the power of concentration."

Eklavya

Near to Dronacharya's *ashram* where the Pandavas and the Kauravas lived while they learnt various arts, lived a small bright boy. His name was Eklavya. Eklavya was very talented and had a keen interest in archery. He wished to learn the art of archery from Dronacharya. But he belonged to shudras, a very low caste. His mother had warned him that Guru Dronacharya would never accept him as his student because he was a shudra. She said that it was useless to dream of ever having that opportunity.

But Eklavya was determined. He said, "I have

accepted Dronacharya as my guru. I shall learn archery from him and no one else." He set up a clay idol of Dronacharya and he worshipped it as his *guru*.

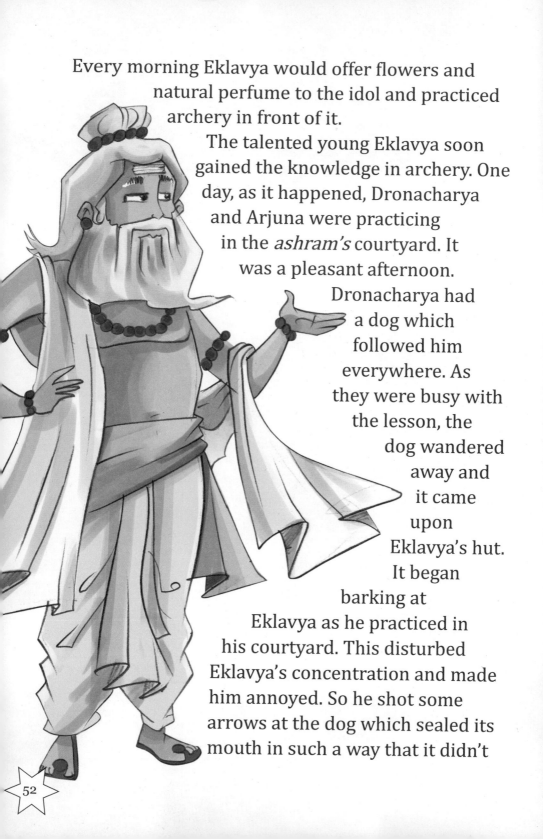

Every morning Eklavya would offer flowers and natural perfume to the idol and practiced archery in front of it.

The talented young Eklavya soon gained the knowledge in archery. One day, as it happened, Dronacharya and Arjuna were practicing in the *ashram's* courtyard. It was a pleasant afternoon. Dronacharya had a dog which followed him everywhere. As they were busy with the lesson, the dog wandered away and it came upon Eklavya's hut. It began barking at Eklavya as he practiced in his courtyard. This disturbed Eklavya's concentration and made him annoyed. So he shot some arrows at the dog which sealed its mouth in such a way that it didn't

hurt it but at the same time made it unable to bark anymore.

The dog ran back to its master for help. When Dronacharya saw his pet's condition he was shocked. He thought, "Only a very skillful archer can do this. As far as I know only Arjuna is capable of such skill. I must find out who this other person is." He asked the dog to lead him to the man who had done it and the dog lead Dronacharya and Arjuna to where Eklavya was practicing.

Dronacharya was amazed at Eklavya's skill. He went to Eklavya and said, "Young man, who has taught you such wonderful skills in archery? Who is your *guru*?"

Seeing Dronacharya in front of him, Eklavya was overjoyed and said, "Why, *gurudev*, all this is your grace! I worship you as my *guru*. I see you in that idol over there. Bless me *gurudev* that I can grow up to be a great archer."

Dronacharya was pleased with Eklavya's dedication. But he was afraid that Eklavya might grow up to be a greater archer than his beloved student Arjuna. He said, "I bless you my son. But as is customary, won't you give me my fees, my *guru dakshina*?"

Eklavya was overwhelmed to see Dronacharya had accepted him as his student. He said, "*Gurudev*, whatever you ask, this humble student of yours will try his best to offer you as *guru dakshina*. I am blessed that you have agreed to be my *guru*."

Guru Dronacharya said, "Son, I am pleased with your devotion. As my *guru dakshina* I want the thumb of your right hand."

The wind stopped in surprise and the trees around stood still. Even Arjuna was stunned on hearing the unusual and almost cruel demand of his *guru*. To ask for the thumb of an archer was equivalent to almost killing him. Without the thumb, Eklavya would never be able to do archery again. Dronacharya had made the demand of such a heavy prize from one disciple to protect the honour of the other.

But Eklavya did not protest. Cheerfully, he drew out his dagger and cut his right thumb. He then placed it at Dronacharya's feet and bowed respectfully. Gods in the heaven silently praised the greatness of Eklavya's sacrifice. Such was his love for his teacher.

The Terrible Oath

Once, the Astha Vasus or the eight deities who assisted Lord Indra had plotted to steal the celestial cow called *kamadhenu*. But they were caught and cursed by Maharshi Vasishtha that they would be born on the earth as humans. The Vasus fell at Vasishtha's feet and begged that he spared them from having to lead the miserable life of humans. Vasishtha said, "I cannot take back my curse but seven of you shall not have to live as humans for long as your mother would kill you soon

after you are born. But Prabasha, you were the one who suggested to the others that they should steal *kamadhenu*. You are the most evil. You shall have to continue to live as a human for a long time." So the eight Vasus were born to Goddess Ganga and the brave king Shantanu who ruled Hastinapur.

Once, while hunting, king Shantanu was passing by the banks of river Ganga on his horse. Suddenly his eyes fell on a beautiful woman. She was so beautiful that the king fell in love with her at once. Mesmerized by her beauty,

he asked her, "Who are you?" The woman replied, "I am Ganga."

The king asked Ganga to marry him but Ganga said she would only marry the king if he agreed to make a promise to her. The king agreed and Ganga said, "Promise me that you will never question my actions. No matter what I do you shall never demand an explanation for it. If you did so, I shall leave you forever."

The king was so blinded by his love for Ganga that he promised and Ganga became his queen after a royal wedding. For many days they lived happily. Then Ganga gave birth to a little boy. The king's joys knew no bounds. But one night, Ganga drowned the baby in the river. The king saw it. But since he had promised his wife that he wouldn't question her actions he did not say anything.

Ganga continued drowning her new born sons in the river. Though this made the king very sad, he was bound by the promise and was forced to not question his wife's strange habit. After seven sons had been drowned, when Ganga took her eighth son to the river the king could not hold his curiosity any longer. He followed her and just as she was about to lay the child in the water he stopped her. He said, "Do not drown my son. I have been quiet for so long but I can't bear to see you kill my sons like this."

Ganga was taken by surprise. She said, "King, the

seven sons I killed were the seven Vasus who were cursed by Rishi Vasishtha. I killed them so that they may be released from the curse. But you have broken your promise. Now I must leave you. I am taking this son with me. He will come back to you once he has grown up." Then Ganga disappeared into the river with the child.

King Shantanu was very sad for many years. Then one day he saw a very handsome boy by the side of the river. The boy was practicing archery. The king was astonished to see that the boy could make the waves of the river Ganga go back with his arrow. He asked the boy, "Who are you?" The boy said, "I am the son of Ganga."

King Shantanu brought the boy to his palace and named him Devavratha. Devavratha's education was well taken care of. Vedas were taught to him by Maharshi Vasishtha. Guru Shukracharya and Brihaspati taught him politics while Parashurama taught him archery. Soon Devavratha mastered the arts and his fame spread to kingdoms near and far.

Once, King Shantanu was strolling on the banks of river Yamuna. He saw a beautiful young woman. The king immediately wished to marry her. Her name was Satyavati and she was a fisherman's daughter.

When the king went to Satyavati's father with the proposal; the fisherman refused it. He said, "Great king, you already have a son who would be the king after you. My daughter's sons will not have any right to the throne. If you promise me that you will not give the throne to Devavratha then I will have my daughter marry you." The king was bound by his duty towards his son Devavratha. So he could not make the promise to Satyavati's father. Heartbroken, the king returned to his palace. Devavratha asked his father about that which had made him so sad, but the king did not answer him.

Devavratha found out from the courtiers that the king wanted to marry Satyavati but was turned away by her father. Devavratha went to Satyavati's father and said, "If that is your condition then I promise you, I shall never ask for the throne. Satyavati's children shall rule after they are of age."

At this the fisherman said, "But what if my grandson is born incapable of ruling?" Devavratha said, "In that case I promise to help him with the matters of the kingdom and shall forever remain at the service of whosoever would sit on my father's throne."

But the fisherman was still not satisfied. He said, "Even if you give up your throne, your children might fight with my grandson's children for the throne." Devavratha replied, "Do not worry. I hereby take an oath that I shall never marry."

The fisherman agreed to marry his daughter to king Shantanu and Devavratha came back to his father with the good news. King Shantanu was amazed at Devavratha's devotion. He was so pleased that he blessed Devavratha with a boon that Devavratha shall live as long as he wished. Devavratha lived a long life. Because of his promise to Satyavati's father he was later called as Bhishma which means 'he of the terrible oath'. According to Mahabharata, in the great battle at Kurukshetra, Bhishma was the supreme commander of the Kaurava forces. He is often considered as a great example of devotion and sacrifice.

Story of King Harischandra

Long ago, king Harischandra ruled the great city of Ayodhya. His wife Taramati has given him a son who was named Rohit. The king ruled his kingdom with wisdom and people loved him for he cared about them.

People often mentioned how wonderfully generous the king was. They said, he had never

turned away anyone who came to him with a wish. One day Rishi Vishwamitra came to his court. The king got down from his throne and bowed to the great sage. Rishi Vishwamitra said, "Great king, I have heard that you do not turn away anyone who comes to you with a wish. Are you ready to sacrifice anything to fulfill my wish?" The king said that he would sacrifice anything. So Vishwamitra continued, "As *dakhshina*, I wish for your kingdom. Will you give it to me?" The king bowed to Vishwamitra at once and said, "Yes lord, it is all yours. I will leave the palace with my wife and son today."

But Vishwamitra was not satisfied. He said, "You must pay me some amount in order to make this *dakshina* effective." But King Harischandra had already given everything he had to Rishi Vishwamitra. He sold his wife and his son to a *brahmin*, who then used them as his slaves. The king sold himself to a guard at a crematorium.

Days passed. Taramati and her son Rohit served the *brahmin's* household as servants. They

lived in a miserable condition. One day Rohit went
to the garden to pluck some flowers. Suddenly he
was bitten by a snake. Rohit died instantly. When his
mother found him she grieved for her son. She took
him to the crematorium to perform his last rites. But
she had no money. When the guard's servant asked
her to pay the tax, she lowered her eyes and stood
silently. It was dark inside the crematorium and

Taramati did not know that the guard's servant was
none other than her own husband. Harischandra
too did not recognize his wife. He said, "If you do
not have money to pay the tax, why don't you sell
that golden *mangalsutra*?" *Mangalsutra* is a sacred
thread women wear around their neck as a symbol
of their marriage. The queen had a boon that apart
from her husband, no one else would be able to see

her *mangalsutra*. No sooner Harischandra had said this Taramati knew it was her husband. She told him of their son's death. The king too grieved for his beloved son. Taramati had nothing but her *saree*. She covered her son's body with half of her *saree* and gave the other half to her husband as tax.

At this, the Gods descended from the heavens and blessed them. Lord Vishnu returned Rohit's life and said, "Great king, we have been testing how true to your virtues you were and we are very impressed by your actions. We return your kingdom and grant that you may now go to heaven." Harischandra said that he could not as he was still bound to his master, the guard. The Gods told him that the guard was none other than Lord Yama, the God of Death. Then Harischandra said, "In that case, I am still bound to my kingdom as king. How can I go to heaven leaving all my people behind?" The Gods refused saying that it was their "*karma*" that has to decide whether they would go to heaven.

Then the king said, "In that case, I will give up my virtues and religiousness so that my people may go to heaven leaving me behind." The Gods were indeed impressed by Harischandra's character. They granted that king Harischandra and all his people may go to heaven after their death.

Churning of the Ocean

Rishi Durvasa was a powerful sage. Though he was a very learned man, he would get angry too quickly. Once, Lord Indra, with all the other Gods, was travelling around the earth on his elephant. They came across Durvasa Rishi's *ashram*. The *rishi* offered the lord a special garland of flowers. Lord Indra put the garland on his elephant's trunk thinking the elephant would put it around its neck. But the mischievous animal threw the garland on the ground. This made Durvasa Rishi very angry. He said, "How dare you insult me like that? I hereby curse you and all the Gods that you would lose your glow and powers."

In the days that followed, Asuras and Daityas began to create troubles for the Gods. Finally, tired of suffering, the powerless Gods went to Lord Vishnu and explained their problems. They said, "Lord, help us find a way. If this continues soon all of us will be killed by the Asuras and the Daityas."

Lord Vishnu said, "You must do a churning of the ocean. The nectar or *amrita* that the churning would yield is the only thing that can restore your powers. But you must seek the help of the Asuras and

Daityas for this." So Lord Indra went to the king of Daityas, Daityaraj Bali. He said, "Daityaraj, with the blessings of Lord Vishnu, we must do a churning of the ocean for which we will need your help. We promise to share with you the gems that will come out from the ocean in the process."

The greedy Asuras agreed to help the Gods in churning the ocean. A meeting was held and it was decided that the mountain Mandrachal would be

used as a churner and Nagraj Vasuki, the king of the
snakes would be wound around the mountain and
pulled from both sides to make the mountain move.

Some Gods and Asuras went to bring the
Mandrachal mountain. But it was so heavy that
they were unable to move it. So they went to Lord
Vishnu and begged him for help. Lord Vishnu flew
on Garuda and lifted the mountain and he brought
it down in the ocean.

But Mandrachal began to sink. Lord Vishnu then turned himself into a giant turtle and swam under the mountain to support it. This giant turtle was called Kurma and was one of the incarnations or *avatar* of Lord Vishnu. The mountain rested on the turtle's back was now ready to be moved. Vasuki was brought and wound around the mountain. The Asuras and Daityas took its head while the Gods took the tail and they began to pull. The mountain began to move and started churning the ocean with it.

First came *Halahal*, the poison, from Vasuki's mouth. The poison began to spread on the earth killing many plants and innocent animals. Since neither of the Asuras, Daityas or Gods were ready to take the poison, they went to Lord Shiva for his help. Lord Shiva took the poison and stored it in his throat. His throat turned blue because of it. That is why Lord Shiva is also called *Neelkanth.*

The churning continued. Then came *Kaamdhenu*, the celestial cow. It was gifted to the sages by Lord Vishnu. Then a horse appeared. It was called *Ucchashrava*. Daityaraj Bali, claimed it for himself. After that came the white elephant with four tusks. It was called *Eravat* and was claimed by Lord Indra for himself. The fifth gift that rose from the ocean was *Koustabhmani*, the most valuable jewel in the world. Lord

Vishnu took it for himself as he was helping with the churning.

After sometime, the tree called *parijata* appeared from the ocean. The Gods took it to heaven with them. Then appeared *Rambha*, a beautiful maiden who herself decided that she would live partly on earth and partly in heaven.

The churning continued and then appeared *Goddess Lakshmi*, the Goddess of

wealth. Both the Asuras and the Gods began fighting amongst themselves for her. But Lord Vishnu said, "Goddess, it is you who must decide who you want to be with." Goddess Lakshmi said, "Neither the Asuras, nor the Gods. I would be your wife and be with you if you have me." So Lord Vishnu took Goddess Lakshmi as his wife.

The next thing that the churning produced was *Varuni*, an alcoholic drink. The Asuras gladly accepted it.

At last, *Dhanvantari*, the doctor of the Gods appeared with the nectar of immortality or *amrita*. All the Asuras, Daityas and the Gods started fighting for nectar. As they fought one of the Asuras grabbed the vessels and started to run. Seeing the confusion Lord Vishnu decided to help them and he turned into a beautiful apsara called Mohini.

Mohini began to dance with the pot of *amrita* in her hand. Gods, Asuras and Daityas sat awestruck and looked at her while Mohini distributed the *amrita*. Then she magically exchanged the pot of *amrita* with a pot of water while she danced so that the Gods drank the real pot while the Asuras and the Daityas got to drink from the fake one. So, Gods became immortal whereas the Asuras and the Daityas were tricked as they drank water instead of the nectar of immortality.